SPECIAL FORCES IN ACTION

W9-CEA-166

Photo Credits

page 10: Granger Collection • *page 11:* Hulton Archive • *page 24:* Hulton Archive • *page 31:* AP Photo • *page 34:* Hulton Archive
All other photos courtesy of the U.S. Army, U.S. Navy, U.S. Air Force, and U.S. Marine Corps

Incorporated

Copyright © 2002
Kidsbooks, Inc.
230 Fifth Avenue
New York, NY 10001

All rights reserved including the right of reproduction in whole or in part in any form.

Manufactured in Canada

Visit us at www.kidsbooks.com

This book is not authorized or sponsored by the U.S. Army, Navy, Air Force, or Marine Corps or anyone involved with them.

SPECIAL FORCES

IN ACTION

by
Tim O'Shei

Consultant:
C. Todd Claus
Former Pararescueman

Contents

Invisible Warriors

You see them in movies. You hear about them in songs. You read about them in newspapers, or in books like this one. But do you actually see them? Not when they are doing their job.

The special forces of the United States military may as well be called "invisible forces." Working best in shadows and darkness, often in groups small enough to fit into a single helicopter, they accomplish amazing feats that an army several times larger could not. From rescuing hostages to demolishing terrorist camps, special forces perform operations that can cripple an enemy and clear the way for full-scale battles.

Real-life Superheroes

Take someone with the strength of Superman and the combat skills of a Jedi knight from *Star Wars*: That is what you get in a special operations soldier. As you learn about the men of the special forces (U.S. law doesn't allow women to fight on the front lines), you will be amazed at the gut-wrenching training and careful preparation they face for every mission.

Army Rangers

Army Rangers can march for days without food or sleep. On a moment's notice, they can spring into an awesome attack.

Green Berets

Army Special Forces, known as **Green Berets,** can hide in the brush of a jungle with an unsuspecting guard standing so close that they can smell his sweat. Using small lasers, they can guide aircraft in the sky toward key bombing targets.

Navy SEALs

Navy SEALs can scuba dive by night to a beach, set up large explosives, then disappear into the water before anyone realizes that they were there. The only clue will be an explosion that blinds the enemy. The SEALs, meanwhile, will have moved on to the next mission.

PJs

Pararescuemen, or "PJs" (short for "parajumpers"), can jump from 30,000 feet and parachute to the ground without ever being noticed. Once they land, they slip through enemy fire to save the lives of fellow Americans and their allies.

Force Recon

Marine Force Reconnaissance teams—"Force Recon"—can hike hundreds of miles into hostile territory and scout the enemy's strengths and weaknesses. They generate a detailed report, complete with photographs, that is provided to a full platoon of Marines who are ready to attack.

Hunting Down Terror

After the attacks on the United States on September 11, 2001, President George W. Bush told Americans that the U.S. military would strike back. He also said that Americans would never hear about some of the missions that were being carried out. These missions had to be kept secret to protect the country and defeat terrorism.

Secret missions like those are the job of the special forces. Few people will ever learn the full story of every operation. However, what we do know tells us this: Long before the September 11 attacks took place, U.S. special-operations teams were preparing to hunt down terror and terrorists. On the following pages, you will learn how they prepare and the methods they use.

When you see the special forces—and even when you don't—you can be sure that they are spread around the planet with one common goal: protecting America.

ARMY RANGERS

HISTORY

Francis Marion is known as the "Swamp Fox." During the American Revolution, he led a militia called Marion's Brigade.

A Long History

Rangers are soldiers (calle light infantrymen) who launc fast, hard attacks, clearing th way for larger groups of troop to move into battle. Like figh ing machines, Rangers ca carry heavy loads of equipme for miles and miles witho food or sleep. Ignoring the bodies' pain, they focus the minds on their mission.

The first modern battalion Army Rangers wasn't forme until June 1942. However, th skills they use have been deve oping for more than 300 years.

In some of the earliest wars American colonial history, sma troops of men fought usin Ranger methods. During Kin Phillip's War (1670-1675), Cap tain Benjamin Church's Ranger fought with Native American along the frontier. In the Frenc and Indian War (1756-1763 Major Robert Rogers forme nine units of Rangers, teachin the troops to be focused an prepared for battle at all times Today's Rangers learn thos same lessons.

Along with Marion's Brigad (who often acted independent Washington's Army), a group Rangers called Morgan's Rifle men helped the colonies wi independence. Rangers als were used in the War of 181 and by the Union and Cor federate armies in the Civil Wa

If you have studied American history, you may know of Francis Marion—the "Swamp Fox." From 1780 to 1783, during the American Revolution, Marion formed an army of men called Marion's Brigade. While hiding in Carolina swamps, these men cut off important messages sent among British commanders, launched surprise attacks, and stopped colonial Loyalists from helping the British. Their actions helped General George Washington's army win America's independence. History books may not mention that Marion and his men were among the first Army Rangers.

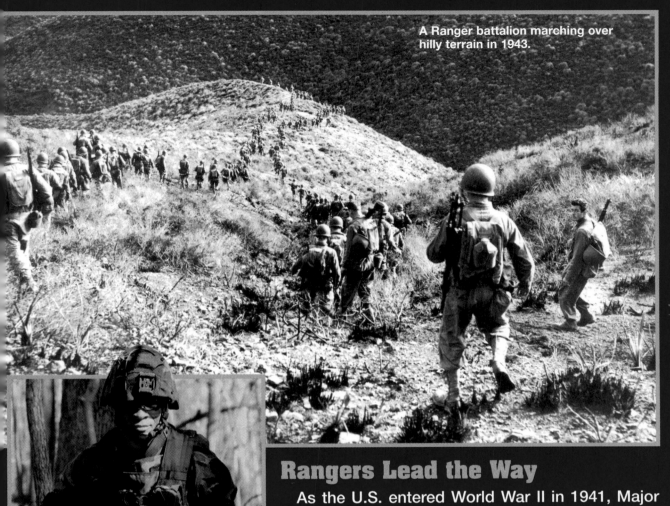

A Ranger battalion marching over hilly terrain in 1943.

Rangers Lead the Way

As the U.S. entered World War II in 1941, Major William O. Darby activated the 1st Ranger Battalion. His men and other Ranger battalions played a key role in helping the U.S. and its allies stop Nazi leader Adolf Hitler from taking over Europe. Operating in Europe and against Japan in Asia, Ranger battalions participated in everything from reconnaissance work to hand-to-hand combat. They even rescued allied prisoners of war.

During the 1944 D-Day landings at Omaha Beach in Normandy, France, the 5th Ranger Battalion was fighting alongside the 29th infantry division. During the bloody beach battle, the commander of the infantry realized that the troops needed to move inland. He commanded, "Rangers, lead the way!" Those Rangers did lead the way that day, and on many others. Those four words—"Rangers, lead the way!"—now stand as the unit's official motto. From the Korean War to the Vietnam War to Operation Enduring Freedom, the Army Rangers have never stopped leading the way.

A U.S. Ranger student in full gear, ready to lead the way.

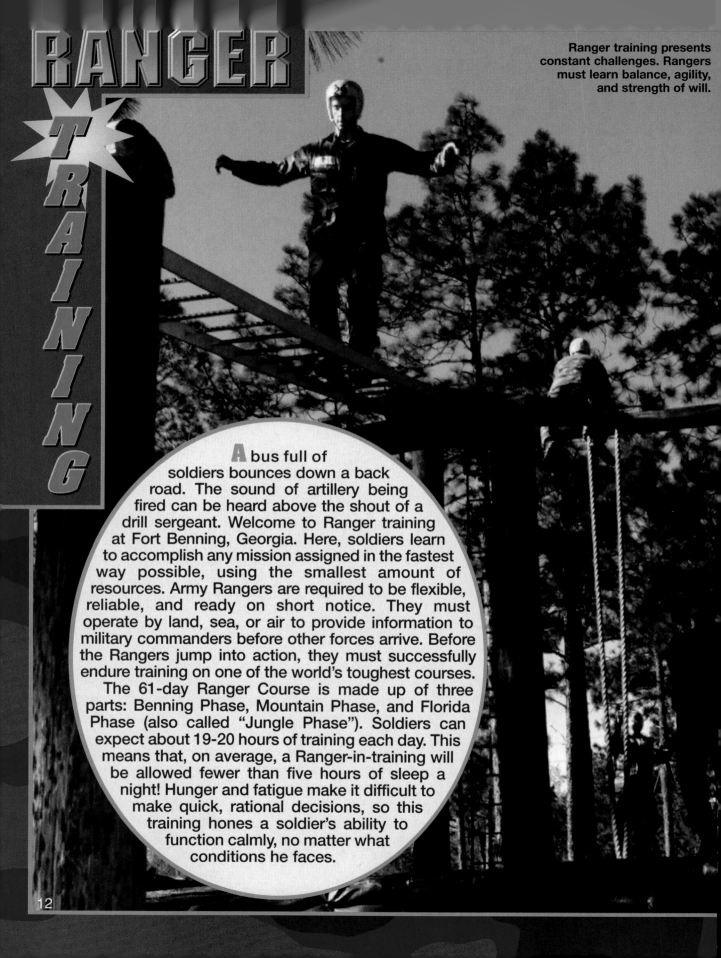

RANGER TRAINING

A bus full of soldiers bounces down a back road. The sound of artillery being fired can be heard above the shout of a drill sergeant. Welcome to Ranger training at Fort Benning, Georgia. Here, soldiers learn to accomplish any mission assigned in the fastest way possible, using the smallest amount of resources. Army Rangers are required to be flexible, reliable, and ready on short notice. They must operate by land, sea, or air to provide information to military commanders before other forces arrive. Before the Rangers jump into action, they must successfully endure training on one of the world's toughest courses.

The 61-day Ranger Course is made up of three parts: Benning Phase, Mountain Phase, and Florida Phase (also called "Jungle Phase"). Soldiers can expect about 19-20 hours of training each day. This means that, on average, a Ranger-in-training will be allowed fewer than five hours of sleep a night! Hunger and fatigue make it difficult to make quick, rational decisions, so this training hones a soldier's ability to function calmly, no matter what conditions he faces.

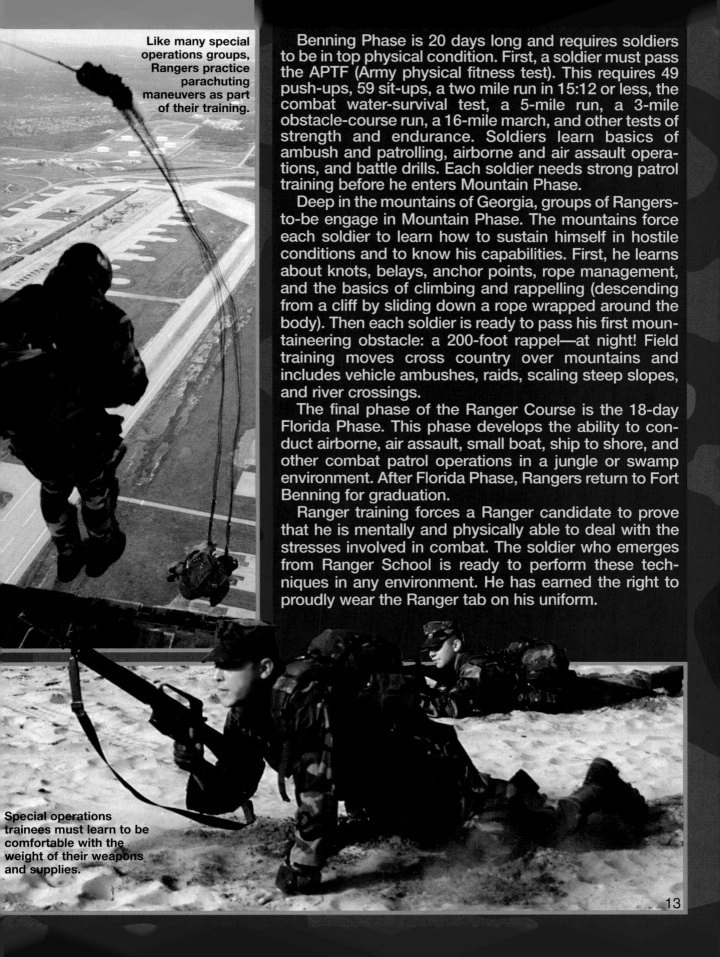

Like many special operations groups, Rangers practice parachuting maneuvers as part of their training.

Benning Phase is 20 days long and requires soldiers to be in top physical condition. First, a soldier must pass the APTF (Army physical fitness test). This requires 49 push-ups, 59 sit-ups, a two mile run in 15:12 or less, the combat water-survival test, a 5-mile run, a 3-mile obstacle-course run, a 16-mile march, and other tests of strength and endurance. Soldiers learn basics of ambush and patrolling, airborne and air assault operations, and battle drills. Each soldier needs strong patrol training before he enters Mountain Phase.

Deep in the mountains of Georgia, groups of Rangers-to-be engage in Mountain Phase. The mountains force each soldier to learn how to sustain himself in hostile conditions and to know his capabilities. First, he learns about knots, belays, anchor points, rope management, and the basics of climbing and rappelling (descending from a cliff by sliding down a rope wrapped around the body). Then each soldier is ready to pass his first mountaineering obstacle: a 200-foot rappel—at night! Field training moves cross country over mountains and includes vehicle ambushes, raids, scaling steep slopes, and river crossings.

The final phase of the Ranger Course is the 18-day Florida Phase. This phase develops the ability to conduct airborne, air assault, small boat, ship to shore, and other combat patrol operations in a jungle or swamp environment. After Florida Phase, Rangers return to Fort Benning for graduation.

Ranger training forces a Ranger candidate to prove that he is mentally and physically able to deal with the stresses involved in combat. The soldier who emerges from Ranger School is ready to perform these techniques in any environment. He has earned the right to proudly wear the Ranger tab on his uniform.

Special operations trainees must learn to be comfortable with the weight of their weapons and supplies.

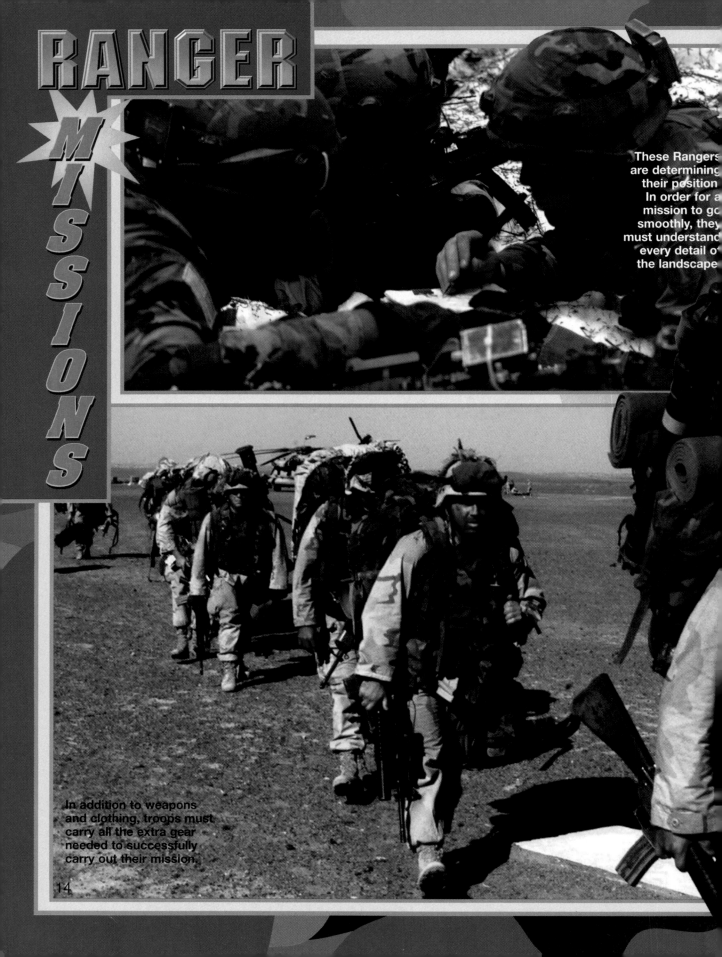

RANGER

MISSIONS

These Rangers are determining their position. In order for a mission to go smoothly, they must understand every detail of the landscape.

In addition to weapons and clothing, troops must carry all the extra gear needed to successfully carry out their mission.

On a dark night in October 2001, a group of about a hundred Army Rangers carefully checked their gear.

"M4 carbine gun?"
"Yes."
"Night-vision goggles?"
"Check. "
"Hand grenade launcher?"
"Got it. "
"M-9 Beretta pistol? K-Bar fighting knife?"
"Both in hand."

Rangers must often work secretly in the night. These troops are wearing night-vision goggles on their helmets.

As the Rangers strapped into their regular equipment, many of them safely tucked in one more item—a photograph. The photo had been taken on September 11. It showed New York City fire fighters struggling to save lives as the World Trade Center's twin towers burned and collapsed. Tonight, October 19, the Rangers and other special-operations forces were in Pakistan. They were about to fly into Afghanistan, home of the Taliban government that had supported Osama bin Laden and his Al Qaeda terrorists. The special-op forces' plan was to raid Kandahar, Afghanistan, to pursue the Taliban leader, Mullah Muhammad Omar. The photos tucked inside their fatigues reminded them why they were there. On September 11, terrorists had killed thousands of people and scared millions more. They had taken their shot. Now it was the Rangers' turn.

Just Dropping In . . .

The Rangers and other troops boarded helicopters and MC-130 Combat Talon planes. Some troops traveled to a spot south of Kandahar. They took control of a dry-lake airstrip and destroyed a stockpile of enemy weapons. Other Rangers traveled directly to Kandahar, dropping in by parachute. They searched for Omar. Although they didn't find him, they were able to gather valuable information to share with their commanders.

Just hours after their entry, the Rangers and other U.S. troops boarded aircraft and took off. They headed back to secure land in Pakistan. Before the sun had risen, they were gone. Rangers like to say, "We own the night." They believe that nobody is better at executing a detailed operation in darkness. On that night in Afghanistan, the Rangers accomplished what they do best: Strike hard, strike fast, and get out.

Although the Rangers were gone quickly from Afghanistan that evening, they surely would be back soon. In the meantime, no clear clues revealed that the disruption and destruction in Kandahar had come at the hand of U.S. soldiers.

No clues except one: Wherever the Rangers went, they left behind one of those New York City fire fighter pictures. It was a simple message to the enemy: America will not give in to terror.

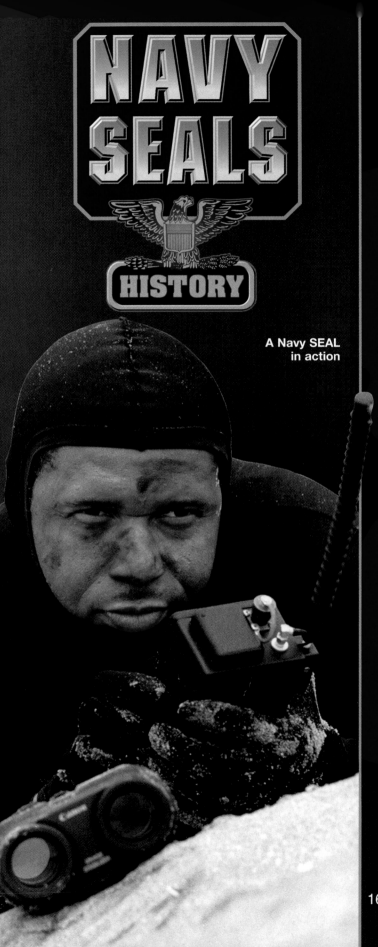

NAVY SEALS
HISTORY

A Navy SEAL
in action

On November 20, 1942, less than a year after Japan attacked the U.S. military base in Pearl Harbor, several hundred U.S. Marines attempted to land on the Japanese island of Tarawa. As the fighters tried to move to the shore, however, they encountered a jagged coral reef hidden beneath the water. Japanese troops fired on the trapped Marines, killing hundreds of them, largely because the landing area on the beach had not been checked for hazards.

The military learned a lesson that day. Never again would troops be sent ashore without a team of experts checking for safe routes ahead of time. In 1943, some of the best men from the Naval Construction Battalions joined the newly formed Navy Combat Demolition Unit (NCDU). These men learned how to swim and run while carrying explosives and equipment through all types of weather. In other words, they could operate anywhere, anytime.

In six-man teams, NCDU members would take a small boat ashore just before an invasion. They would find a safe path and map out the enemy locations before a full force of Marines would move in.

During the war, the Navy created larger groups of these sailors, called frogmen. They formed 100-man underwater demolition teams (UDTs) that checked shores for danger. One key place was off the beach of Normandy, France. The Germans had placed concrete blocks, steel spikes, and barbed wire underwater to keep Allied ships from moving in. It was the job of the frogmen to find these obstacles and destroy them.

By the end of World War II in 1945, there were 34 UDTs. Frogmen worked again during the Korean War (1950-1953). That time, they also worked on land, checking harbors and rivers for mines. Jumping from airplanes and parachuting to the ground, frogmen destroyed enemy bridges, tunnels, and railroads.

SEALing Vietnam

In the 1960s, each branch of the U.S. military developed a special-force unit with its own specialties. In 1962, the Navy chose its first teams of SEALs (SEa, Air, Land) using

JDT sailors. SEALs were trained to conduct secret missions in any environment. Although they could combat any type of enemy, SEALs were specially trained in guerrilla warfare methods.

That training was valuable when the SEALs were sent to Vietnam. Working in thick jungle, SEALs used the rivers and coasts to slip behind enemy lines. From here, they launched surprise attacks on Viet Cong camps. They destroyed weapon and food supplies and took prisoners. After the U.S. withdrew from Vietnam in the early 1970s, the SEALs were given new responsibilities. One of those was fighting terrorism—a challenge that still exists today.

Parachuting is an important skill, since SEALs must be comfortable in any environment.

These SEALs are preparing an underwater vessel for use. They are well trained in scuba diving.

SEALS TRAINING

These SEALs are practicing their exits from a hovering helicopter. SEALs must learn to move quickly and with confidence.

From sea to air to land, there is no place on Earth where the Navy SEALs cannot operate. SEALs can parachute from airplanes by night, undetected. With barely a rustle, they can slither through jungle or across desert. They can scuba dive below the surface of dark, murky waters, hidden from all enemies above.

Underwater warfare is a specialty of the SEALs. Like all special forces, SEALs are invisible warriors. Their bodies can do things that you would expect only from a high-tech machine. To become SEALs, young Navy men undergo nearly a year of gut-wrenching physical training. Most men who enter the BUD/S (Basic Underwater Demolition/SEAL) program never finish. The few who do become some of the most elite warriors on the planet.

Welcome to BUD/S

Any male Navy member who is 28 or younger is welcome to apply for BUD/S training to become a SEAL. (Occasionally, a 29- or 30-year-old is accepted.) Two screening tests are administered. A medical test ensures that the candidate has good eyesight and health. A physical-screening test, which consists of swimming, push-ups, sit-ups, pull-ups, and running, shows whether the candidate can meet the minimum fitness level for BUD/S.

SEAL candidates first participate in a five-week instruction course, which teaches them about the training and, if they make it through, the job. After this course, candidates take a more advanced physical test. Those who pass advance to First Phase.

Starting Out

First Phase of BUD/S is eight weeks of physical conditioning and skills training. Candidates complete four-mile runs in boots, two-mile swims in fins, and timed obstacle courses. The third week is often called Hell Week, because candidates train for five-and-a-half days, getting only four hours of sleep—total! The only way to survive Hell Week is through teamwork. Many candidates drop out during this period. Those who make it through have proven their physical and mental strength, so they move on to skills training—such as mapping and charting water areas—for the next five weeks.

Working with military groups from many countries allows broad training for the SEALs. Here, SEALs are training with members of the Singapore Navy.

rom Water to Land

After First Phase, candidates move on to cond Phase—eight weeks of diving truction, training them to become combat immers. They also continue the running, -mile swim, and obstacle-course training. During Third Phase—nine weeks of land-rfare training—they learn how to attack by d and use weapons and explosives both ove ground and under water. Candidates actice their new skills—such as detonating plosives—on San Clemente Island (owned the Navy) off the coast of California.

inally a SEAL!

After completing the three phases, andidates spend three weeks in para-hute instruction and 15 weeks in SEAL ualification training. After that, success-ul candidates become certified SEALs. ypically, they are assigned to one of two eams, on either the east coast (Virginia) r west coast (California).

SEALs enjoy a rare moment of rest while riding to the next practice site. They often train in camouflage to simulate actual conditions.

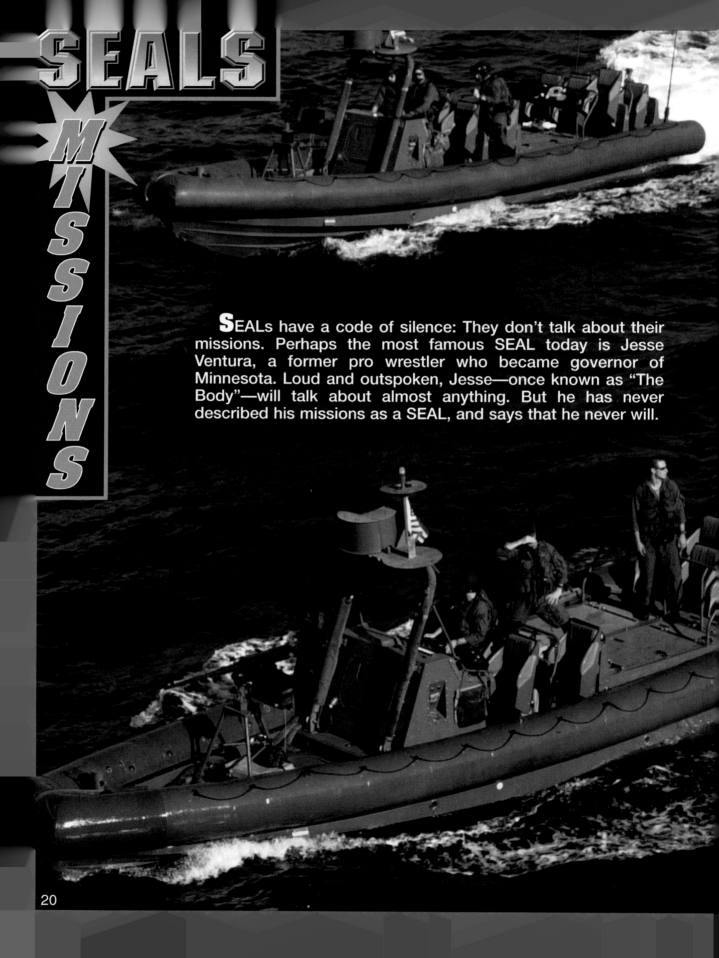

SEALS
MISSIONS

SEALs have a code of silence: They don't talk about their missions. Perhaps the most famous SEAL today is Jesse Ventura, a former pro wrestler who became governor of Minnesota. Loud and outspoken, Jesse—once known as "The Body"—will talk about almost anything. But he has never described his missions as a SEAL, and says that he never will.

SEALs exiting a CH-53 "Sea Stallion" near their camp in Bosnia.

SEALs can function anywhere, but are at home on the water.

Silent and Dangerous

Not all SEAL missions are total mysteries. During the Persian Gulf War in 1991, for example, a team of six SEALs played a key role in tricking the Iraqis into expecting an invasion from sea. The SEALs team swam ashore to a Kuwaiti beach, set explosives on a timer, then retreated back into the water. At 1 a.m., the beach exploded in a brilliant flash.

From the water, the SEALs added machine-gun fire and more explosives. The Iraqi military, thinking that they were about to be invaded from the sea, sent two divisions of troops to the beach. Meanwhile, the U.S. and its allies invaded Kuwait from the ground. Thanks to the crafty work of the SEALs, the invaders faced fewer Iraqi troops. Tricked by the SEALs, two Iraqi divisions had left the front lines and headed toward an empty beach.

These SEALs discovered weapons and ammunition while conducting a Sensitive Site Exploitation (SSE) in the mountains of Afghanistan.

SEALS

MISSIONS

A digital camera can send real-time images to decision makers via satellite.

Weaponry and More

SEALs are trained to use a variety of deadly tools, from submachine guns to grenade launchers to rockets, but like to think of themselves as the most dangerous weapon. Not only are they physically fit and mentally strong, they can also make themselves practically invisible. On the ground, they can hide in brush and blend into landscapes. In water, they can ride close to shore using SEAL delivery vehicles, then scuba dive the rest of the way.

SEALs even have a method for invisible scuba diving: When necessary, they use a closed-circuit breathing system, a device that recycles exhaled air, removing the carbon dioxide. (In open-circuit scuba diving, exhaled air bubbles to the surface, which may give the enemy a clue that someone is coming.)

A SEAL gives the "OK" sign while working underwater with a SEAL delivery vehicle (SDV). These vehicles are used for nearly silent underwater travel.

To Be a Navy SEAL

In recent years, Navy SEALs and other special forces have adopted high-tech equipment that helps them do their jobs better and faster.

For example, a SEAL may crawl along the base of a mountain in the middle of the night. He carries a digital camera, laptop computer, night-vision goggles, and weapon. Upon finding his target—maybe a makeshift terrorist camp—he aims and shoots, but not with a gun. His weapon is the camera. He sends the image via satellite from his computer to a command center. The command center sends the image to an attack plane. Within minutes, the plane drops a bomb on the target, destroying it cleanly and completely. With another day's work done, the SEAL slips back into the darkness.

On board a barge in the waters off Afghanistan, SEALs search for contraband and Al Qaeda troops.

ARMY GREEN BERETS

Special Forces played a large role in the Vietnam War.

HISTORY

The year was 1941, and the United States was on the brink of World War II. A rich American lawyer named William "Wild Bill" Donovan advised President Franklin D. Roosevelt that the U.S. needed a new military agency. Donovan—who happened to be a hero of World War I—wanted the U.S. to form a special operations group that would send spies and warriors into enemy territory. These brave troops would steal secrets and launch surprise attacks on the enemy.

The OSS

Roosevelt agreed. He asked Donovan to create an agency that became known as the Office of Strategic Services (OSS). The OSS sent three-man teams into Europe. They trained local men from allied countries to fight against the Germans. The OSS forces focused on slowing the German army by destroying railroads, oil refineries, and power plants. In Asia, OSS soldiers trained 11,000 Burmese tribesmen, who then attacked enemy Japanese soldiers.

Donovan's vision of a small, sleek, and threatening unit had become reality. The OSS was shut down after World War II, but its work lived on when the Special Forces was formed in 1952.

Special Forces trained men in guerilla-fighting techniques similar to those taught by the OSS. While the Rangers specialized in mounting quick surprise attacks, then retreating, the Special Forces were trained to live inside enemy territory. They spied on the enemy, collected information, and mapped the land. They also trained local people to be guerrilla fighters. Their mission was to remain invisible, silently breaking down the enemy's defenses.

The Green Beret

During the 1950s, Special Forces units developed into 12-man groups known as A-teams. Each A-team had members who specialized in intelligence, weaponry, communications, medical care, or engineering. This gave the A-teams

A Green Beret in full combat gear, including a binocular headpiece for careful searching in the brush.

a variety of skills that they could use anywhere in the world.

In 1953, members of one A-team began wearing a green beret. Other A-teams followed suit, and the beret became popular. The Army officially adopted it in 1961, when President John F. Kennedy called the beret "a symbol of excellence, a badge of courage, [and] a mark of distinction in the fight for freedom." Since then, the Special Forces have become better known as the "Green Berets."

Green Beret soldiers in uniform

GREEN BERETS

TRAINING

Special Forces trainees must crawl under barbed wire with all their gear. Often, live ammo is fired over the area to simulate combat conditions.

Soldiers who want to become Green Berets begin by volunteering for a three-week program called the Special Forces Assessment and Selection (SFAS). In the first week, candidates speak with a psychologist, who checks their mental fitness. They also undergo physical-fitness testing. This includes swimming in gear and boots and marching 150 miles while carrying 50 pounds of equipment and a weapon.

Week two requires candidates to work their way through a mile-and-a-half obstacle course and do more marching. They are given three chances to pass "Star," an 18-kilometer land-navigation course. Star requires a soldier to make his way through hills and swamps at night, without a flashlight, through all kinds of weather.

In week three, soldiers are formed into teams and given group tasks, such as moving a large trailer without wheels several miles. Judges are always watching, looking for the soldiers who demonstrate the best leadership and problem-solving skills.

Usually, about half of the candidates flunk the SFAS program. Those who pass receive parachute and leadership training before going on to the Special Forces Qualification Course (SFQC).

Developing a Specialty

The first step of the SFQC is the individual skills phase. It is a 40-day program during which candidates learn about land navigation and the special tactics of a small, 12-man unit. After that, soldiers pick their specialty. Choices are as follows:

• **Weapons specialists** learn about U.S. and foreign weapons. They can assemble and take apart almost any weapon or land mine—a useful skill when surrounded by enemies. (*training time: 24 weeks*)

• **Engineer specialists** learn how to

nstruct essential structures, such as ridges or shelter. Engineers also learn ow to use demolition explosives. (*training time: 24 weeks*)

Medical specialists become highly killed paramedics. They are able to perform some kinds of surgery and help oldiers who have suffered trauma in attle. (*training time: 57 weeks*)

Communications specialists become xperts in radio-wave and satellite communications. Prospective "Commo" specialists are sent more than 1,000 miles way from their training center in North arolina and must find their way back to nish their communications training. (*raining time: 32 weeks*)

Detachment Commanders learn leadership skills. They are good planners and rectors. (*training time: 26 weeks*)

arning the pecial Forces Tab

After specialty training, all Special orces candidates enter a final field st called Exercise Robin Sage.

No strangers to heights, soldiers learn balance, agility, and confidence in any situation.

In Exercise Robin Sage, candidates put together their creativity, fighting skills, and specialties to work as a team. When they finish, they have finally earned the Special Forces tab. They go on to receive training in one of 12 foreign languages and are assigned to a permanent unit, where they continue to receive specialty training.

Soldiers practice maneuvers in a simulated combat situation.

GREEN BERETS

MISSIONS

Map reading in the deserts of Afghanistan.

Green Berets are trained in weaponry, parachuting, rappelling, and scuba diving, like other special operations troops. But another weapon sets them apart: their minds.

Green Berets are a brainy group. Many of them have college degrees, and they tend to be older (often in their 30s) than other special operations troops. Each Green Beret speaks a foreign language. He is expected to learn about the culture of the country in which he works. Often, part of a Green Beret's job is to blend into the country and seem like he belongs there as a native. Deep inside enemy territory, Green Berets train local people in guerrilla warfare.

Teachers in War and Peace

When the U.S. launched Operation Enduring Freedom shortly after September 11, 2001, the Green Berets sprang into action. Many of their missions may remain secret forever, but at least one has been made public. In early November, an A-Team of 12 Green Berets and an Air Force combat controller landed in the icy mountains of northern Afghanistan. Their mission was to find a specific Northern Alliance commander, and train him and his fighters. Together, the Green Berets and these Northern Alliance soldiers would try to gain control of a city called Mazar-e Sharif from the Taliban.

Trying to blend in, the A-team members had grown beards before arriving in Afghanistan. They didn't sleep for two days as they moved toward the camp with 200 pounds of equipment. Once there, they struggled to find a common language. Finally, they discovered that one of the Berets and one of the Afghan men spoke Russian. At last they could communicate.

Green Berets duck out of the way of a landing plane. They are prepared to unload soldiers and supplies.

After much discussion, the Afghan group led the U.S. troops on a day-long trip. They arrived at a camp of 2,000 Northern Alliance soldiers who were hungry and cold. The Green Berets called for an airdrop. Soon, food, blankets, clothing, and ammunition were falling from the sky. Now happy with the Americans, the Northern Alliance troops were ready to fight.

Led by the Green Berets, the troops moved north toward Mazar-e Sharif. When they came across a Taliban town or camp, the group called in air strikes. The soldiers used lasers to point aircraft toward the targets. By the time they got to the city, Taliban troops were already fleeing. As the A-team arrived in Mazar-e Sharif, they were greeted by crowds of cheering citizens. The citizens were thanking them like heroes for driving the soldiers away.

The Berets had not imagined that they would win the town so quickly. But their job wasn't done. For months, that A-team remained in Mazar-e Sharif, focused on another part of a Green Beret's job: keeping the peace.

A team of Green Berets in Colombia, training Colombian troops to help stop the export of drugs.

AIR FORCE PARARESCUEMEN

MISSIONS AND HISTORY

If you witnessed a car accident, what would you do? You probably would call 9-1-1. Soon, an ambulance would rush to your location with the sirens blaring. The medics inside would be ready to help. The Air Force has its own version of a special-rescue unit, but these life-saving experts don't travel by ambulance. Rather, they leap from planes into some of the most dangerous territory on Earth.

Meet the PJs

Pararescue specialists are trained to do exactly what their name suggests: They jump from an airplane by parachute or descend from a helicopter by cable, and rescue injured troops. Called PJs, these airmen are highly trained medical specialists. They specialize in saving the lives of pilots and other special operations forces dur-

ing combat. From a plane soaring 30,000 feet above ground, they parachute to a precise location. They ca do it on any type of land, from the jungles of Vietnam t the frozen Arctic to the mountains of Afghanistan. water is in the way, no problem: PJs can scuba div while carrying more than 100 pounds of equipment.

Well trained in rescue and survival techniques, PJ can move undetected through enemy territory. The find injured or stranded troops or pilots, administe whatever immediate medical help is needed, the move the patient back to safety. Patients are ofte transported by helicopter, but PJs will move them b any transportation available.

First Mission

The first pararescue teams date back to World Wa II. In 1943, a C-46 aircraft flying above the borde between Burma and China was about to crash. Twenty one people parachuted to safety. They landed in a jur

Pararescuemen usually arrive by helicopter, but they will move patients by any means necessary.

Above: In 1997, a pararescue team searched the crash site of an A-10 warplane that went down near Vail, Colorado.

Below: Here, a Pararescueman treats a wounded soldier.

e that had no paths or roads. An Army Air rce Lieutenant Colonel named Don eckinger offered to parachute into the jungle h two enlisted medical corpsmen. They und the 21 men, treated their wounds, and them to safety.

In 1947, the Air Force was split from the my and became a separate branch of the itary. More pararescue teams were med. During the Korean War in the early 50s, the Air Force had as many as 45 ven-person pararescue teams working to U.S. and allied soldiers.

By the late 1950s and into the 1960s, the Force employed fewer pararescue teams. e PJs of that era began working with NASA well as with other special forces, such as Green Berets. PJs continue to work with er special operations units today.

Toward the end of the 1960s, with U.S. forces fighting in the jungles of Vietnam, the role of the PJs grew. Using new rescue techniques that incorporated helicopters, PJs were able to save more than 4,000 lives. More than half of those rescues occurred in combat situations. The Pararescuemen truly lived up to their motto: "These things we do that others may live."

31

AIR FORCE PARARESCUEMEN

TRAINING

Pararescuemen practicing parachuting.

Pararescuemen we maroon berets that stand f "sacrifice." Not only do P sacrifice their own safety order to help others, but airm also must undergo tremendo sacrifices to earn the privile of wearing the maroon beret.

Passing the Test

When candidates enter t Pararescue/Combat Cont Indoctrination Course Texas, they must pass t Physical Abilities and Stami Test. Within three hours, th must:
• swim four laps of 25 mete underwater and 25 meters the surface in under 8 minute
• swim 1,500 meters in minutes, 30 seconds.
• run 3 miles in 22 minutes, seconds.
• perform 10 chin-ups in minute.
• do 75 sit-ups in 2 minutes
• complete 50 push-ups in minutes.
• do 60 flutter kicks in minutes.

Flying Forward—or Falling Back?

Airmen who pass the phy cal test move forward in t Indoctrination School. "Indo is a 10-week course design to screen candidates. It wee out everyone who can't ha dle the physical and men demands of the job. Anywhe from 70 to 90 percent of t trainees who start the cour fail to finish it. Once they dr out, they return to active du elsewhere in the Air Force.

After Indoc, candidat move to the U.S. Army A

an area. In HALO parachuting, a PJ jumps from a plane flying at an altitude of 30,000 feet. He free-falls at roughly 200 feet per second, steering himself in midair by slightly moving his arms or legs. Somewhere between 2,500 and 3,500 feet from the ground—or about two minutes and 20 seconds into his free fall—the PJ pulls the rip cord on his parachute and floats safely to the ground. PJs parachute this way to slip into enemy territory or to rescue an injured person. It is necessary when the injured person is somewhere unreachable, like a ship or the side of a mountain.

The opposite of HALO is HAHO—high-altitude, high-opening parachuting. In HAHO parachuting, the jumper opens his parachute at 28,000 feet and may float down slowly for over an hour while steering his way to the landing zone.

After parachute training, candidates learn combat medical techniques and become nationally registered paramedics. The final step to becoming a Pararescueman is the Pararescue Recovery Specialist Course. The yearlong training school includes academics and practical training in many geographical environments. This prepares PJs for the areas they may have to enter. After a year of learning how to perform dangerous rescues, successful students officially become Pararescuemen—trained and ready to save lives.

Three pararescuemen come in for a HALO landing during exercises with the British Special Air Services.

orne School at Fort Benning, Georgia, to earn parachuting techniques. Next, they ttend Combat Divers School in Key Vest, Florida, to learn to scuba dive with eavy equipment.

Candidates must attend schools where hey learn how to escape from sinking ircraft, survive in the wilderness, and se evasion techniques that help them ide from enemies in hostile territory.

Free-fall Jumping

One of the most important skills that a J learns is HALO parachuting (HALO tands for "high-altitude, low-opening"). lso called free-fall parachuting, it is an xciting, though dangerous, way to enter

This pilot is using a map to check the location of his helicopter during a drop-off exercise.

MARINE FORCE RECONNAISSANCE

A Marine wades through a river during the Vietnam War.

When a professional football team has a Sunday game, it doesn't just charge onto the field and play. The athletes have spent all week preparing for this one game. They have studied a game plan and perfected special plays designed to plug the enemy offense and plow through the opposing defense. A good football team enters its Sunday clash fully prepared physically and mentally.

Military operations are much more serious than football games, so detailed preparation is even more vital. Troops do not simply burst into battle. They plot and prepare, pinpointing the enemy's weaknesses and learning about the land, water or airspace where their part of the battle is likely to take place.

Like football players, warriors plan as a team, but someone else provides the information that allows them to prepare. In football, that information comes from scouts—people who watch other teams play and write detailed reports about what they saw. In the U.S. Marine Corps, delivering such valuable information is the job of the Force Reconnaissance team—Force Recon, for short. Force Recon teams are often the first troops to enter a dangerous place where battle is about to take place. They find safe landing spots, clear away obstacles and, if necessary, become deadly fighters.

The Early Recons

During World War II, the Marines' reconnaissance battalion began working with the Navy's UDTs, scouting water and beach areas to provide safe landings for larger groups of fighters. Working mostly in four-man teams, Force Recon provided on-site help for the military during five different World War II battles.

During the Korean War, Force Recon worked alongside UDTs again, blowing up tunnels and bridges to hinder the enemy's ability to travel.

Seen through a night-vision lens, this Force Recon Marine is staying low to the ground. Soldiers move undetected more easily at night. They scout an area and provide information to the rest of the military.

Like other special operations units, Force Recon found itself busy during the Vietnam War, aiding troops in the jungle environment. While Force Recon worked in seven-man units in Vietnam, teams grew as large as 23 men each in the years that followed.

More Than Just Scouts

Searching and spying are two key Force Recon talents. While they excel at providing information through charts and photographs, they also are completely prepared to do battle. The first helicopter assault in the history of the Marines occurred under the control of Force Recon, during the Korean War.

Force Recon members are trained to recover downed pilots, rescue prisoners, conduct underwater searches, and hustle hostages back to safety. All of this is done deep behind enemy lines. Force Recon makes that happen by living its three-word motto: "Swift. Silent. Deadly."

MARINE FORCE RECONNAISSANCE

Force Recon Marines on a light armored vehicle (LAV) prepare to go on patrol.

The work of a Recon Marine is nearly unnoticeable. Unlike the Green Berets or SEALs, who are so well-known that they have been the subject of movies, most civilians have never heard of Force Recon.

That is fine with the Recons themselves. They believe that they form one of the best special operations units in the world. They don't do it for the glory, they say. They do it for their country.

Wide-ranging Training

How does a person become a Recon Marine? First, he has to enlist in the U.S. Marine Corps and attend basic training, called boot camp. From there, he can request to be enrolled in Force Recon training. The first sergeant or sergeant major of a platoon also can recommend qualified men for Recon school. (As with the other special operations units, U.S. law allows males only.)

Once a Marine enters Recon training, he receives instruction in a variety of skills and techniques. He learns advanced parachuting skills, aircraft-control operations, demolition techniques, communications, and photography. Recons in training also learn how to

These Force Recon Marines are arriving at a site in Afghanistan. They are traveling in a CH-46 Sea Knight helicopter.

...age battle in any situation. They are trained in combat ...cuba diving, assault climbing, and mountain warfare. ...orce Recon candidates learn special skills for fighting ...verywhere from jungles to city settings. Some are sent to ...niper school, where they learn to become sharpshooters. ...y the time a Recon Marine has finished with his training, ...e not only knows how to scout out and prepare an area ...r invasion and battle, he also is an expert in fighting.

Breaking Enemy Lines

When U.S. military forces invaded Grenada in 1983, ...orce Recon was there. Six years later, Recons played ...heir part in Operation Just Cause, in which special forces ...ntered Panama to seize the dictator and drug lord, ...eneral Manuel Noriega. The operation was successful: ...oriega was captured and brought to the United States, ...here he was tried and convicted for drug trafficking.

In 1991, after Iraq had invaded its neighbor, Kuwait, ...orce Recon helped lead the way again. After detailed ...urveillance of the Iraqi front lines, Recons identified the ...nemy's weak spots and pointed the Marines to them. It ...ok only weeks for the U.S. and its allies to drive Iraq out ...f Kuwait. For that quick, clean, and effective operation, ...e military had the special operations—including Force ...Recon—to thank.

Like many other special operations groups, Force Recon Marines are trained in rappelling. Rappelling allows them to move safely up and down the side of a mountain, cliff, or even ice.

OTHER SPECIAL OPERATIONS TEAMS

Army Delta Force

In the 1970s, America's attention was drawn to terrorist attacks around the world. The U.S. Army needed a group that could counter such attacks. The 1st Special Forces Operational Detachment-Delta (SFOD-D), a counterterrorist group which became known as Delta Force, was formed.

Since its beginning in 1977, Delta Force has successfully participated in many operations, including Operation Just Cause in Panama in 1989, the Persian Gulf War in 1991, and Operation Enduring Freedom, which began in 2001.

The operations of Delta Force are covert, so little is known about the unit or its involvement. In fact, the U.S. military does not officially recognize the Delta Force in any way. For an antiterrorism unit like Delta Force, secrecy is key.

SEAL Team Six

The other U.S. counterterrorism unit, SEAL Team Six, is nearly as secretive as Delta Force, but its existence is well-known. The founder of Team Six, Commander Richard Marcinko, is one of the most famous SEALs.

Team Six was created shortly after a botched hostage-rescue attempt in 1980. It was made up of SEALs who received extra training in counterterrorism techniques. Over the years, they have been active in rescue missions and terrorism-prevention tasks. For example, they helped secure Panamanian leader Manuel Noriega during Operation Just Cause in 1989. Team Six is now called "Dev Group," which is short for Naval Special Warfare Development Group.

Combat Control Teams (CCTs) set up communications they will need to control air traffic. CCTs are also responsible for securing an airport or creating a landing strip for friendly planes.

Army Night Stalkers

When the Army Rangers or Green Berets are deployed on a mission, somebody has to fly them to the target. That job belongs to the 160th Special Operations Aviation Regiment (Airborne), which is called SOAR(A) for short. The job of this unit is to provide aerial support for Army special operations.

SOAR(A) was formed in the early 1980s, shortly after Operation Eagle Claw failed in its mission to rescue U.S. hostages being held in Iran. U.S. military officials realized that aviation specialists were needed.

Working with the Rangers and Green Berets, SOAR(A) has flown many missions at night. That earned the battalion its nickname, the "Night Stalkers."

Night Stalkers sometimes use the HH-60G helicopter for search and rescue, infiltration, exfiltration, and resupply of special operations forces in day, night, or difficult weather conditions.

Air Force Combat Controllers

The job of the Combat Control Teams (CCTs) is to be "First There" and make sure that an area is safe for friendly planes to fly and land. Often working alongside other special operation units, CCTs move in ahead of the other units to secure an airport or create a landing strip. (If a plane needed to land in a field, for example, it is the Combat Controllers' job to sweep it for mines, remove trees and logs, and set up landing markers.) They have expertise in explosives, communication techniques, and air-traffic control.

CCTs specialize in HALO and HAHO parachuting as well as scuba diving. Much of their training is completed alongside Pararescuemen. Together, CCTs and PJs form the Special Tactics Team of the U.S. Air Force.

Special Boats Units must be familiar with many high-tech water vehicles. These sailors are working in an AAV (amphibious assault vehicle).

Navy Special Boat Units

Sailors who make up the Navy's Special Boat Units (SBUs) are called Combatant Crewmen. Their job is to help SEALs infiltrate (move into) and exfiltrate (move out of) a site. Like SEALs, Combatant Crewmen undergo heavy physical and mental training. As expert sailors and navigators, they can operate quickly and quietly in both oceans and rivers, and in deep or shallow water. Well-trained in weaponry and survival techniques, the Crewmen are always battle-ready.

Would You Like to Join the Special Ops?

Does special operations work sound exciting? Do you think that you have what it takes to work among the world's most elite warriors? If you think you do, here are some things you need to know.

Chow Down, But Chow Healthy!

Members of U.S. special forces follow strict diets—for instance, no junk food and no muscle-building supplements. Here is a partial list of foods that the Navy recommends to its special operations trainees:

- **boiled eggs**
- **tuna fish**
- **lean meats**
- **fresh fruits and vegetables**
- **peanut butter**
- **breads and cereals**
- **yogurt, milk, and other dairy products**

There are strict rules about diet—even about what kind of Gatorade or PowerAde a soldier can drink! (Single-serving packages are the only type allowed.)

Work Out!

An effective special operations soldier is strong and fit. You can start your training by taking part in aerobic activities that you enjoy, such as running, swimming, and bicycling. Team sports can also provide an intense workout, so consider basketball, baseball, hockey, football, or soccer, among others. But, remember that muscles need time to rest. Start your routine slowly and begin to build on it as your endurance increases.

If you would like more information on exercise routines, talk with the physical education teacher at your school. He or she can help you plan a routine that suits your needs.

Follow Those Rules!

If you break a rule in school, what happens? If it's a small rule and you don't get in trouble often, probably not much. Breaking bigger rules, of course, leads to bigger consequences.

In the special forces, you cannot break *any* rules, big or small. In the handbook given to Ranger hopefuls, there is a section called "Most Common Mistakes in SFAS" (Special Forces Assessment and Selection). Among the mistakes the Army advises soldiers to avoid are:

- failing to give 100-percent effort
- whining
- losing your temper
- constantly sitting down first or getting up last during a break
- falling asleep (unless you are in bed)
- not following instructions
- cheating
- being negative
- giving up on anything

Members of U.S. special forces are taught things that can help them even after they leave the military. Among the most useful lessons they learn are survival skills. If you were ever to get stranded on a deserted island, you would want a Ranger, Beret, SEAL, PJ, or Recon with you!

Skills that special ops learn include:

- how to turn anything that moves into a meal.
- how to collect water by wrapping a plastic bag around a tree branch and leaves. (Water evaporating from the leaves condenses in the bag.)
- how to communicate using anything from a radio to signal fires to a mirror. (You can use mirrors to reflect sunlight and get the attention of a plane flying overhead.)
- how to build a shelter out of almost anything.

An excellent book containing information on these skills and many others is *Castaway Survivor's Guide* by Rory Storm (Scholastic Inc., © 2000)

How Much Do You Know?

A Special Operations Quiz

1. What did the Rangers leave behind after their strike in Kandahar, Afghanistan?

2. What is an A-team?

3. Which U.S. president helped the Army's Special Forces get their nickname, the Green Berets?

4. Frogmen are associated with which special operations group?

5. What does SEAL stand for?

6. What is a PJ?

7. What is the name of the parachuting technique in which a person jumps from 30,000 feet but doesn't pull his rip cord until he is 3,500 feet from the ground?

8. Which two special operations groups specialize in scouting an area before a large number of troops attack?

9. Which special operations group is responsible for moving Navy SEALs in and out of an area?

10. Which U.S. special operations unit was the first to be formed specifically to counter terrorism?

(See p. 45 for the answers.)

Glossary

battalion: a body of troops made up of 2 to 5 companies or 500 to 1000 people

boot camp: introductory training for most units of the U.S. military

branch: section of the United States military. The five branches of the U.S. military are the Army, Navy, Air Force, Marines, and Coast Guard

BUD/S: Basic Underwater Demolition/SEAL—the training program for Navy SEALs

civilians: people who are not in the military

Combat Control Teams (CCTs): Air Force teams that clear a landing area for incoming friendly planes and provide air-traffic control

commandos: military people who are members of the special forces

covert: veiled or secret

Delta Force: a secret group of U.S. Army special operations soldiers that is not officially recognized by the U.S. government

exfiltrate: to move out of an area

fatigued: to be physically tired

fatigues: the combat uniform of a soldier

Force Recon: The U.S. Marine Corps' special operations group that is responsible for entering an area and providing information about the enemy to other Marine troops

Green Berets: nickname for the Army's Special Forces—a group that specializes in intelligence gathering, guerrilla recruitment and training, and other forms of unconventional warfare

guerrilla warfare: secret military operations in hostile territory conducted by small groups

HAHO: high-altitude, high-opening parachuting in which a jumper opens his parachute at a high altitude (about 28,000 feet) and drifts down slowly

HALO: high-altitude, low-opening parachuting in which a jumper falls quickly, then opens his parachute 2,500 to 3,500 feet from the ground

infiltrate: to move into an area

Night Stalkers: nickname given to the 160th Special Operations Aviation Regiment (Airborne). Night Stalkers provide aerial support for Army special operations.

OSS: the Office of Strategic Services. Created under President Franklin D. Roosevelt, the OSS was active during World War II.

pararescue: part of the Air Force special tactics team, Pararescuemen are medical specialists who enter the site of an incident by land or air to rescue survivors

Rangers: an Army special operations group that specializes in quick, surprise attacks

rappelling: descending from a cliff by sliding down a rope wrapped around the body

reconnaissance: the gathering of information about people or a place

scuba: an underwater diving technique; *scuba* stands for "self-contained underwater breathing apparatus"

SEAL: a Navy special operations group that works in the sea, in the air, and on land

SEAL Team 6: a Navy counterterrorism group that is now called "Dev Group"—Naval Special Warfare Development Group

sniper: a gunman trained to hide while aiming for specific, often hard-to-reach targets

Special Boats Units (SBUs): a Navy special operations group that helps SEALs move in and out of a site by boat

Special Tactics Team: U.S. Air Force special operations forces that consist of combat control, pararescue, and combat weather teams

UDT: underwater demolition team

Quiz Answers
(see p. 42)

1. The Rangers left behind photographs of New York City fire fighters taken at the World Trade Center disaster site.

2. An A-team is a group of 12 Green Berets. Each member has a special skill, including intelligence, weaponry, communications, medical care, or engineering.

3. President John F. Kennedy. He called the beret "a symbol of excellence, a badge of courage, [and] a mark of distinction in the fight for freedom" when the beret was adopted in 1961.

4. Frogmen are associated with the Navy SEALs. Before teams of SEALs were formed in 1962, frogmen were underwater demolition experts.

5. SEAL stands for SEa, Air, Land.

6. A PJ is a Pararescueman, who is capable of parachuting down to rescue wounded pilots and soldiers. PJ is short for "parajumper."

7. HALO. It stands for high-altitude, low-opening. Using this parachuting maneuver, a jumper waits until he is 2,500 to 3,500 feet from the ground before pulling the rip cord and floating safely to the ground.

8. Marine Force Recon and Combat Control Teams. Marine Force Recon is responsible for scouting an area before a large number of troops attack. Air Force Combat Control Teams also scout the area, to assure that there is a clear landing space for incoming aircraft filled with troops.

9. The Navy Special Boats Units are responsible for infiltrating and exfiltrating SEALs.

10. Delta Force. It was the first U.S. special operations unit formed specifically to counter terrorism.